Elementary

Just

Reading and Writing

For class or self-study

Carol Lethaby
Ana Acevedo
Jeremy Harmer

With Geraldine Sweeney

Marshall Cavendish
Education

Photo acknowledgements

p.6 ©Heide Benser/zefa/Corbis; p.7 a ©Holger Scheibe/zefa/Corbis, b ©Veronique Beranger/zefa/Corbis, c ©Jason Horowitz/zefa/Corbis, d ©T. Kruesselmann/zefa/Corbis; p.8 1 ©Stanley Chou/Getty Images, 2 ©Robyn Beck/AFP/Getty Images, 3 ©Daniel Berebulak/Getty Images, 4 ©Reuters/Cobris, 5 ©Jussi Nukari/Rex Features, 6 ©Juan Carlos Munoz/Getty Images, 7 ©Antonio Scorza/AFP/Getty Images, 8 ©Ciniglio Lorenzo/Corbis Sygma; p.10 ©Moodboard/Corbis; p.11 t-b ©Flint/Corbis, ©Charles Gullung/zefa/Corbis, ©Jose Luis Pelaez,Inc./Blend Images/Corbis, ©image100/Corbis; p.12 l-r ©Ingram Publishing/Alamy, ©Joe McNally/Reportage/Getty Images, ©Helene Rogers/Alamy, ©Rob Crandall/Stock Connection/Alamy, ©Corbis, p.16 ©Inti St Clair/Digital Vision/Getty Images; p.17 ©PCL/Alamy; p.19 ©Moodboard/Corbis; p.23 ©Peter Bennett/Rex Features; p.25 ©Nicolas Russell/Iconica/Getty Images, ©Nicolas Russell/Iconica/Getty Images; p.26 l ©Ferruccio/Alamy, r ©Benno de Wilde/Imageshop/Alamy; p.31 ©Bob Thomas/Stone/Getty Images; p.32 t ©Hisham Ibrahim/Photographer's Choice/Getty Images, b ©Cosmo Condina/Stone/Getty Images; p.33 t ©Helen King/Corbis, b ©Chad Ehlers/Alamy; p.38 ©virgo/zefa/Corbis; p.41 a ©Robert Slade/Manor bPhotography/Alamy, b ©Geoffrey Taunton/Sylvia Cordaiy Photo Library Ltd/Alamy, c ©Andrew Parker/Alamy; p.44 1 ©Craig Lovell/Corbis, 2 ©Julie Eggers/Corbsi, 3 ©Charles O'Rear/Corbis; p.46 t ©AA World Travel Library, b ©AA World Travel Library; p.47 ab ©I. Glory/Alamy, b ©PhotoSpin, Inc/Alamy, c ©PhotoSpin, Inc/Alamy, d ©Stockbyte Silver/Alamy, e ©PhotoSpin, Inc/Alamy, f ©Ablestock/Hemera Technologies/Alamy, g ©Stockbyte Silver/Alamy; p.48 ©Mephisto/Rex Features; p.49 ©Nils Jorgensen/Rex Features; p.52 ©Kevin Dodge/Corbis; p.53 a ©Frans Lemmens/zefa/Corbis, b ©Art Wolfe/The Image Bank/Getty Images, c ©Bryan & Cherry Alexander Photography/Alamy; p.59 ©George Gower/The Bridgeman Art Library/Getty Images; p.60 ©Gianni Dagli Orti/Corbis; p.64 ©Owen Franken/Corbis; p.71 ©Purestock/Alamy; p.74 ©Image100/Alamy

© 2007 Marshall Cavendish Ltd
Reprinted 2008

First published 2007

by Marshall Cavendish Education
Marshall Cavendish is a member of the Times Publishing Group

ISBN: 978-0-462-00043-5

Marshall Cavendish Education
5th Floor
32–38 Saffron Hill
London
EC1N 8FH

Designed by Hart McLeod, Cambridge

Printed and bound by Times Offset (M) Sdn Bhd

Contents

●●●● Introduction

For the student

Welcome to *Just Reading and Writing*. You can use this book with other students and a teacher, or you can work alone with it.

In this book, there are 24 units. We have chosen topics which we hope you will find interesting. They include articles, postcards, quizzes, emails and text messages. This book has many practice exercises to help you with reading and writing. Each unit has a section on reading skills. There is then a section on developing your writing skills.

When you see this symbol (🔑), it means that the answers to the practice exercises are in the Answer key at the back of the book. You can check your answers there.

We hope that this book helps you progress in English and, above all, that you enjoy using it.

For the teacher

This book is part of a series to be used alone or to supplement any coursebook you may be using. Each book in the series specialises in either language skills or aspects of the English language. It can be used either in class or by students working on their own.

Just Reading and Writing consists of 24 units, containing a variety of reading texts on subjects such as jobs, sports, lifestyle and travel. These are designed to give students experience of many different types of reading materials and writing tasks. Students will be able to use the exercises even if a teacher is unavailable for explanations or guidance, since there is a comprehensive Answer key. However, the units are also highly appropriate for work in class.

We hope you find this book a real asset and that you will also try the other books in the series: *Just Listening and Speaking*, *Just Grammar* and *Just Vocabulary*.

UNIT 1

WHO ARE YOU?

•A Reading Introducing someone

1 Read the speech bubbles and circle the right expression.

a   *Hi, how are you?* (*I'm Tom. What's your name?*)   Hello. I'm Sally.

b   This is Nicola.   *Not bad, thank you. / Nice to meet you.*

c   Hi, I'm Frank. What's your name?   *I'm Mike. / Pleased to meet you.*

d   Hi, John. How are you?   *Not bad, thank you. / My name's Max.*

2 Read and match the identity badge with the person. Write the full name of the person in the labels *1–4*.

International Conference
Name: Roseni Amorim

International Conference
Name: Elena Petrovich

International Conference
Name: Yoshi Watanabe

International Conference
Name: Charlie Walker

3 Read the conversations again. Write the name of the persons who say each thing.

a What's your name?   *Roseni*

b Not bad, thank you.

c Elena, this is Charlie.

d Nice to meet you too.

e How are you?

f Nice to meet you.

4 Put the caption with the correct picture.

1 Roseni meets Charlie.   [*b*]

2 Yoshi and Elena.   [   ]

3 Roseni, Yoshi and Charlie.   [   ]

4 Charlie, Elena and Yoshi.   [   ]

5 Put the conversation in the right order.

a Hi, Marie. Not bad, thank you.   [   ]

b Brad, this is my friend Dilip.   [   ]

c Are you a teacher, Dilip?   [   ]

d Hi Brad, nice to meet you too.   [   ]

e Hi Dilip. Nice to meet you.   [   ]

f Hello, Brad. How are you?   [*1*]

g No, I'm a student.   [   ]

6 Answer these questions for you.

What's your name?

My name is

How are you?

Are you a teacher?

●●B Writing An email

From: Jerome
To: Tina

Hi Tina!

How are you? I'm Jerome. Here are some photos. David and Ray are my friends. Jane and Jaro are new friends. They're students in my English class. We're at the *Just Right* School of English. Nick is my teacher. Are you in an English class? Who are your friends? Who's your teacher?

Email soon!

Bye!

Jerome

1 Read Jerome's email and label the photos.

2 Read the email again and write True (T) or False (F).

a David and Ray are teachers.   [F]

b Jane and Jaro are students.   [   ]

c Nick is a teacher.   [   ]

d Jerome is a teacher at the *Just Right* School of English.   [   ]

3 Match the questions a–f with the answers 1–6.

a Who are they?   1 I'm Mark.
b Is she a teacher?   2 No, they're Don and Josh.
c Is he a student?   3 Yes, he is.
d What's your name?   4 They're Tina and Elena.
e Are you a student?   5 No, I'm a teacher.
f Are they Dave and James?   6 No, she's a student.

4 Write questions.

a What / name? _____What's your name?_____

b How / you? _____

c Who / your friends? _____

d Are / student? _____

e Who / your teacher? _____

_____

a
.......Jerome.......

b

My friends ....
and ....

c

My new friends ....
and ....

d

My ....
....

5 Write an email to Jerome about you, your friends and your teachers. Ask one question.

From: ....
To: Jerome

Hi Jerome!

I'm ....

....

....

Email soon!

Bye!

....

WHERE ARE YOU FROM?

●●●A Reading Colours, countries and nationalities

1 Look at the words. Put them in the correct list below.

Colours	Countries	Nationalities
grey		

grey ◆ **Mexican** ◆ blue ◆ United Kingdom
yellow ◆ Canadian ◆ **Mexico** ◆ France
French ◆ **Australia** ◆ Japanese ◆ **Australian**
black ◆ **British** ◆ **green** ◆ **white** ◆ red
Canada ◆ Japan

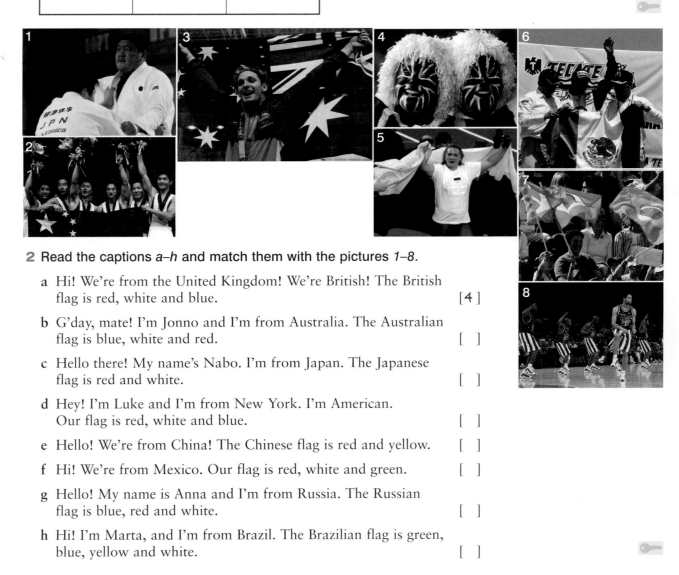

2 Read the captions a–h and match them with the pictures 1–8.

a Hi! We're from the United Kingdom! We're British! The British flag is red, white and blue. [4]

b G'day, mate! I'm Jonno and I'm from Australia. The Australian flag is blue, white and red. [ ]

c Hello there! My name's Nabo. I'm from Japan. The Japanese flag is red and white. [ ]

d Hey! I'm Luke and I'm from New York. I'm American. Our flag is red, white and blue. [ ]

e Hello! We're from China! The Chinese flag is red and yellow. [ ]

f Hi! We're from Mexico. Our flag is red, white and green. [ ]

g Hello! My name is Anna and I'm from Russia. The Russian flag is blue, red and white. [ ]

h Hi! I'm Marta, and I'm from Brazil. The Brazilian flag is green, blue, yellow and white. [ ]

3 Are the sentences True (T) or False (F)?

    a The British flag is red, green and blue.   [F]

    b Anna is Australian.   [ ]

    c The Brazilian flag is green, blue, yellow and white.   [ ]

    d Luke is not from Canada.   [ ]

    e The Mexican flag is red, white and green.   [ ]

    f The Chinese flag is red and blue.   [ ]

    g Marta is not from Mexico – she's Brazilian.   [ ]

4 Write sentences about the people in pictures *1–8*. Use the names of countries and nationality words.

    Example: 1 *They're from Japan. / They're Japanese.*

5 Tick (✓) the correct answers for picture 3.

    a
    - What's his name?
    - His name is Jonno.   [✓]
    - His name is Mike.   [ ]

    b
    - Is he British?
    - Yes, he is.   [ ]
    - No, he isn't.   [ ]

    c
    - Is he Australian?
    - Yes, he is.   [ ]
    - Yes, I am.   [ ]

    d
    - Where is he from?
    - He's from Australia.   [ ]
    - He's from Japan.   [ ]

    e
    - Is his flag red, white and blue?
    - Yes, it is.   [ ]
    - Yes, he is.   [ ]

6 Answer the questions for you.

    a Are you English? *No,*_____

    b Are you American?_____

    c Where are you from? _____

    d Is your teacher from Mexico?_____

    e Where is your teacher from? _____

●●●B Writing A letter

Dear Emma,

How are you? My name's Zak. I live in the USA,
but I'm not American.
My mum's from France and my dad's from
Canada. We live in Westchester. It's near
New York. Are you British? Where are you from?
Is it nice?

Bye!
Zak

1 Read the letter from Zak to his new penpal Emma.
Circle the right answer.

a Zak is (Canadian) / British.

b Zak lives in (Westchester) / New York.

c Zak's dad is from Mexico / (from Canada.)

d Zak's mother is not (Chinese) / French. 🔑

2 Complete the questions Zak asks.

a How _are you_ ?

b Are _you British_ ?

c Where _are you from_ ?

d _Is it nice?_ ? 🔑

3 Read Emma's reply to Zak. Underline Emma's
answers to Zak's questions.

Dear Zak,

I'm very well, thank you. How's it
going for you? I'm British but my dad
is Russian. We're from Bakewell, near
Manchester. My teacher is from
Canada too. And yes, Bakewell is nice.

Bye!
Emma

🔑

4 Write to Zak. Answer his questions. Ask him a question.

Dear Zak,

How are you? My name is ....
I'm from .... It's near ....
I'm .... My mum .... My dad ....
.... ?

Bye!
....

UNIT 3

A Reading Jobs and occupations

1 Match the jobs *a–j* with the places where people work.

| hospital | kitchen | office |
| school | street | theatre |

a cook   ....kitchen....

b doctor   ....

c nurse   ....

d actor   ....

e accountant ....

f taxi driver ....

g singer   ....

h architect   ....

i dancer   ....

j teacher   ....

2 Look at the photos of these four people. Which four jobs do you think they do? Do the puzzle below and write the place where they work and their job. Check your answers in the Answer Key.

| accountant | actor | architect | ~~cleaner~~ | cook | dancer | doctor |
| taxi driver | engineer | nurse | singer | student | teacher |

	Works in	Job
Stephanie	a school	
Alex		
Andrew		
Patrick		

Clues:
a Stephanie is not a cleaner. She works in a school.
b Alex works in a theatre. She's not a singer.
c Andrew doesn't work in an office. He's not a taxi driver.
d Patrick doesn't work in a school. He works in an office.
e Stephanie is not a student or a nurse.
f Alex is not an actor.
g Andrew works in a kitchen. He's not a doctor.
h Patrick is not an accountant or an engineer.

3 Look at Activity 2 again. Are the sentences True (T) or False (F)?

a   Stephanie works in a hospital.   [F]

b   Patrick works in a kitchen.   [   ]

c   A cook works in an office.   [   ]

d   Students and teachers work in a school.   [   ]

e   An accountant works in an office.   [   ] 🔑

4 Say which person from Activity 2 is talking.

a   'Hello. I work in a school, but I'm not a student.' _Stephanie_

b   'Hi! I work in a kitchen. I'm not a cleaner.' ....

c   'Hi there. I work in a theatre, but I'm not an actor.' ....

d   'Hello. I work in an office, but I'm not an accountant.' .... 🔑

baker

dancer

bus driver

computer programmer

painter

5 Look at the pictures. Fill in the blanks in sentences _a–e_ with the correct word.

a   Ben Jones bakes bread. He's a .... _baker_ ....

b   Ellen Brown dances in the theatre. She's a ....

c   Melanie Davis drives a bus. She's a ....

d   Steve Laws programs computers. He's a ....

e   Yusuf Khan paints houses. He's a .... 🔑

6 Answer the questions about your family and friends' jobs and occupations.

My mum's a .... She works in ....

My dad's a .... He works in ....

Our neighbour is .... He/She ....

My boyfriend/girlfriend is .... He/She ....

I'm ....

●●B Writing Form-filling

1 Read the form and write True (T) or False (F).

a Lola is a doctor.   [F]

b Her last name is Jones.   [ ]

c Her email address is morenolola@hotmail.com [ ]

d Her telephone number is 07856 563337.   [ ]

e Lola is Spanish.   [ ]

2 Read the questions. Write Lola's answers.
Which question can you not answer?

a What's your first name? _Lola_ ....

b What's your last name? ....

c How are you today? ....

d Where are you from? ....

e What's your email address? ....

f Do you have email? ....

g What's your telephone number? ....

h What's your job? ....

3 You want information about a driving school. Fill in
the form below for yourself.

HIGHBURY Library

First name
Lola

Last name
Moreno

Nationality
Spanish

Job/Occupation
Computer programmer

Telephone number
07856 563387

Email address
morenolola@aol.com

HAPPY DRIVER Driving School

First name: ....

Last name: ....

Address: ....

Age: ....

Nationality: ....

Email address: ....

Telephone number: ....

Job: ....

UNIT 4
FAMILIES

●●●A Reading Family members

1 How many family words can you find in the wordsearch? Which are male? Which are female?

```
G R A N D M O T H E R
C H U W X O S W I F E
O U N Q V T X O U C U
U S T H E H O V N C N
S B U S I E D W C D C
I A U S B R N D X E L
N N G R A N D S O N E
Q D R S I S T E R H S 🔑
```

2 Read the two texts. Match the texts with the family trees. Then label the pictures with the names of the people.

My name is Jo Smith. I'm a dentist. I'm from Argentina. I have one brother, Alberto. He and his wife Patty have one son, Paco. My husband, Peter, is English. We have two sons, Freddy, 12, and Ricky, eight, and a baby daughter, Monica, 18 months old. [ ]

I'm Joe Smith and I'm 38. I'm an architect. My father is from Scotland and my mother is from Jamaica, in the Caribbean. I'm British. I am an only child. My wife, Sandra, is a teacher. We have two daughters: Alice, 12, and Neisha, six. We also have a son, Barry, 14 months old. We live in England. [ ] 🔑

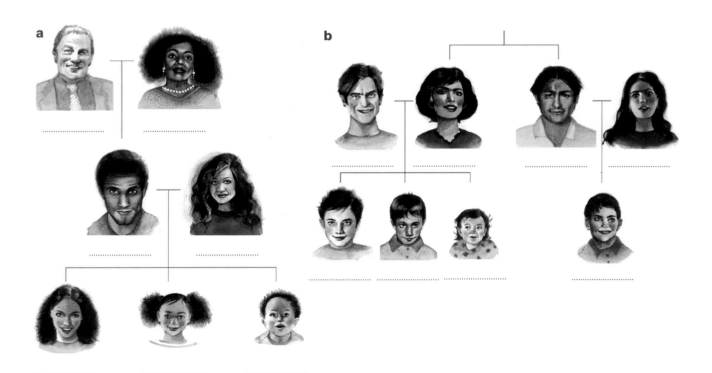

3 Are the sentences True (T) or False (F)?

a Alberto and Jo are brother and sister.   [T]
b Sandra is Joe's wife.   [ ]
c Joe and Sandra have two sons and one daughter. [ ]
d Alberto is Freddy, Ricky and Monica's father.   [ ]
e Jo Smith is an architect.   [ ]
f Monica is 18 years old.   [ ]
g Monica and Barry are brother and sister.   [ ] 🔑

4 Find the words a–g in Activities 2 and 3. Match them with the definitions 1–7.

a mother   1 child (girl)
b father   2 the husband of my mother
c sister   3 child (boy)
d brother   4 the wife of my father
e only child   5 my mother's daughter
f son   6 has no brothers or sisters
g daughter   7 my mother's son   🔑

5 Match the questions a–f with the answers 1–6 about Joe's family.

a How old are you?   [3]

b Who's Sandra?   [ ]

c What's her job?   [ ]

d What's your nationality?   [ ]

e Do you have any brothers or sisters?   [ ]

f How old is your baby son Barry?   [ ]

1 He's 14 months old.
2 She's a teacher.
3 I'm 38.
4 I'm an only child.
5 I'm British.
6 She's my wife.   🔑

6 Answer the questions about Jo's family.

a What's Jo's job? _She's a_ ....

b Where is she from? ....

c Is Jo an only child? ....

d Who is Peter? ....

e How old is Freddy? .... 🔑

B Writing Punctuation and capital letters

1 Look at these sentences. Answer the questions below.

> My name is Jo Smith. I'm a dentist. I'm from Buenos Aires in Argentina. I have one brother, Alberto. He and his wife Patty have one son, Paco.
>
> My father is from Glasgow in Scotland and my mother is from Barbados, in the Caribbean.

a When do we use a capital letter? Tick (✓) the correct box.

For:

1 names of people	[✓]	5 beginning sentences	[✓]
2 countries	[✓]	6 family words	[✗]
3 nationalities	[✓]	7 names of towns and cities	[✓]
4 ages	[✗]	8 pronoun *I*	[✓]

b What do we use at the end of a sentence?

comma (,) [ ]   full stop (.) [✓]   apostrophe (') [ ] 🔑

2 Look at the photo and read the text. Then add the capital letters and full stops.

> hi! i'm ben. this is my family. that's me in the middle i'm chinese but I live in britain
>
> i'm a student. i have two sisters, annie and paula. paula is a nurse. she has three children: ricky, 10, rosie, 3 and pip, 13 months. my grandparents and my aunt and uncle live in the usa. but my cousins are in london .

3 Draw and label your family tree. Write a paragraph (six to eight sentences) about you and your family. Try to answer these questions.

How old are you?

What's your job?

Where are you from?

Where do you live?

Where are your mother and father from? Are you an only child? What is your brother's/sister's job? How old is he/she? Are you married? How old is your son/daughter?

Hi! I'm ....

....

....

....

....

UNIT 5

TIME

•• AReading A pilot's story

1 Work out this problem.

Alan starts work at 8.00 a.m. every Tuesday. He works for 11 hours and finishes work at 11.00 a.m. on the same day. How is this possible?

2 Read the text and check your solution to Activity 1.

A life in the sky

Pilots have interesting lives. They visit many places and meet many people. But is it an easy job?
Alan Alder is a pilot. He usually flies from London to Los Angeles on Tuesdays. He gets up at 5.00 and he arrives at the airport at 6.00. His flight is at 8 o'clock. Eleven hours later he's in California. It is 11.00 a.m. in Los Angeles. Normally, he doesn't go out on the first day. He relaxes: he plays squash, he watches television and goes to bed early. On Friday he flies back to London. Does he like his job? 'It's very hard work,' he says. 'But the money is good and I have good holidays. Life in the sky is great!'

3 Mark the statements True (T) or False (F).

a Alan flies to California on Tuesdays.   [T]
b He gets up very early.   [   ]
c Alan's flight is at 6 o'clock.   [   ]
d Alan spends eight hours in the sky.   [   ]
e Alan goes out on Tuesday night.   [   ]
f Alan spends five days of the week in California. [   ]
g Pilots have easy jobs.   [   ]
h Alan likes his job.   [   ]

4 Read the text again and fill in the blanks.

a Pilots ......visit..... many places and .... many people.

b Alan usually .... to LA on ....

c He .... at 5.00 and he arrives at ....

d Normally, Alan .... on the first day.

e On Tuesday he .... squash, ... TV and

.... early.

f He .... his job. He .... 'Life in the sky is great.'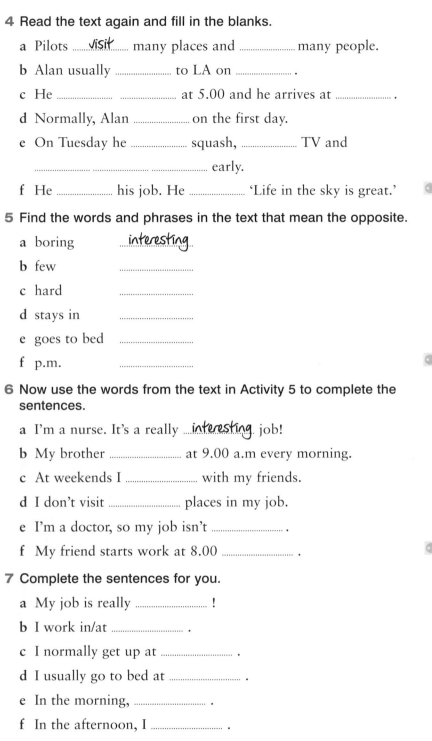

5 Find the words and phrases in the text that mean the opposite.

a boring   ...interesting...

b few   ....

c hard   ....

d stays in   ....

e goes to bed   ....

f p.m.   ....

6 Now use the words from the text in Activity 5 to complete the sentences.

a I'm a nurse. It's a really ...interesting. job!

b My brother .... at 9.00 a.m every morning.

c At weekends I .... with my friends.

d I don't visit .... places in my job.

e I'm a doctor, so my job isn't ....

f My friend starts work at 8.00 ....

7 Complete the sentences for you.

a My job is really .... !

b I work in/at ....

c I normally get up at ....

d I usually go to bed at ....

e In the morning, ...

f In the afternoon, I ....

g At weekends, I ....

●●B Writing You and your job

My name's Jody. I work in an office in Brighton. I'm an accountant. I don't really like my job. I start work every day at 9.00 a.m., so I get up at 7.30 in the morning. I work from 9.00 a.m. for eight hours until 5.00 p.m. I usually go out at lunchtime, eat a sandwich, or read the paper. Normally I don't go out in the evening but on Fridays I meet friends after work. Friday is my favourite time of the week! My least favourite time? Guess! Yes, it's Monday morning …

1 Read the text. Circle the correct answer.

a Jody is *an engineer /* *an accountant.*

b She works *in a hospital / in an office.*

c Jody *likes / doesn't like* her job.

d She gets up every morning at *7.30 / 8.30.*

e Every day, she works for *nine / eight* hours.

f At lunchtime, she usually *goes out / doesn't go out.*

g Her *favourite / least favourite* time of the week is Friday.   🔑

2 Complete the sentences.

a Jody starts work at 9.00 a.m. *every day* .

b She works for eight hours ....

c At lunchtime, she .... goes out.

d Normally she doesn't go out ....

e She meets friends after work ....   🔑

3 What's your job? Are you a student? Do you like it?
Write a short text like the one about Jody in Activity 1.

Hi! My name's ....

....

....

....

UNIT 6

FOOD AND DRINK

●●●A Reading Food shopping

1 What's your favourite food? What's your least favourite food? Write 1 for your favourite food and 12 for your least favourite food. Then write each item in the table below.

cereal [ ]

cheese [ ]

chocolate [ ]

crisps [ ]

eggs [ ]

fish [ ]

fruit [ ]

meat [ ]

salad [ ]

soda [ ]

tea [ ]

tuna [ ]

Food
eggs
Drinks
Snacks

2 Match the words *a–g* with the pictures *1–7*.

a carton [2]

b packet [ ]

c bar [ ]

d bottle [ ]

e can [ ]

f box [ ]

g loaf [ ]

3 Read the labels on the foods *a–f* quickly. Match the labels with the phrases in the box.

> an avocado   a box of cereal   a carton of juice
> a can of soup   a packet of crisps   a can of tuna

a *a box of cereal*

b

c

d

e

f

4 Which food or foods labelled in Activity 3:

a have salt? _crisps, soup, tuna_
b have protein? ....
c have fat? ....
d come from Mexico? ....
e is fruit? ....
f have vegetables? ....
g have no fat? ....
h have olive oil? ....
i is fish? ....

Which product is natural?

5 Read and write True (T) or False (F).

a The soup is dolphin-friendly.   [F]

b The box of cereal contains tomatoes.   [   ]

c The packet of crisps contains nuts.   [   ]

d The carton of juice contains water.   [   ]

e The avocado has proteins, vitamins and natural oil. [   ]

6 Fill in the blanks in the shopping lists below. Use the words from Activity 2 to help you. Then write the correct title for the shopping list.

A: Picnic

B: Breakfast

Shopping list for ....

a 2 bottles of Coke
b 5 .... crisps
c a .... tuna
d a .... bread
e a .... butter
f a .... soda
g a .... eggs
h 5 .... chocolate

Shopping list for ....

a a .... eggs
b a .... cereal
c a .... milk
d a .... bread
e a .... juice

●●●B Writing Cafés and restaurants

1 What kind of food do you like to eat? What is the name of your favourite restaurant?

2 Read the posters and write the name of the restaurant: *Joe's café*, *Dessert Stop* or *Avenue de Paris*.

a Healthy food is their speciality. ....Joe's café....

b They have ice cream cake. ....

c Their food is suitable for vegetarians. ....

d The food is 'take away'. ....

e Fresh fish is their speciality. ....

f The restaurant is open until 2.00 a.m. ....

g They are closed on Wednesday and Sunday. ....

3 Read the posters again and circle the correct answer.

a The *Avenue de Paris* is a *Mexican* / (French) restaurant.

b At *Joe's café* you can eat *healthy snacks* / *desserts*.

c *Dessert Stop* sells *ice cream cake* / *vegetarian food*.

d The French restaurant specialises in *fresh fish* / *chocolate cake*.

e The take-away restaurant sells *apple pie* / *vegetable soup*.

4 Which of the three restaurants do you like best and why?

I like .... best because I like

.... and ....

I don't like .... or ....

5 Write about your favourite restaurant.

My favourite restaurant is ....

It is .... The food is ....

It has .... It's open ....

The speciality of the restaurant is ....

6 Design a poster for a restaurant you know.

UNIT 7

FREE TIME

••A Reading Sports

1 Look at the picture. What is the man's hobby?

a playing football
b watching football
c doing puzzles
d driving a taxi

Read the article and check your answer.

> **A Football Fan**
> Meet Alex McGovern. He's 28 years old, from
> Manchester, and he's a taxi driver. His hobby is
> football and he loves Manchester United.
> He **always** goes to the games at Old Trafford.
>
> What about his family? "He **usually** plays with us on
> Sunday, but he **never** spends Saturday with us," say
> his children, Eric (five) and Amanda (eight). His wife,
> Liz, doesn't like football and she **always** stays with
> the children when Alex is at
> the game.
>
> Are Eric and Amanda football fans like their dad?
> No! They don't like football – they both love
> watching TV and doing puzzles.

2 Read the article again. Are the sentences
True (T) or False (F)?

a Alex is a football player.   [F]
b He likes football.   [ ]
c He never goes to watch
   Manchester United.   [ ]
d Manchester United play at Old Trafford. [ ]
e Alex never plays with the children. [ ]
f The children always spend Saturday
   with Alex.   [ ]
g Liz likes football.   [ ]
h She never goes to the game with Alex. [ ]
i The children always stay at home on
   Saturday.   [ ]

3 Read the questions and write the answers.
Write sentences.

a Where is Alex from? He is from ....

b What is Alex's job? ....

c What sport does he like? ....

d Where are the Manchester United games?

   ....

e Does Liz like football?

   ....

f What do Eric and Amanda like doing?

   ....

4 Look at the words in blue in the text. Check the
meaning and complete this table.

| occasionally | often | sometimes | usually |

More frequent————————————→ Less frequent					
100%	80%	60 – 80%	40 – 50%	10 – 20%	0%
always					never

5 Complete these sentences using the words
from Activity 4. Use all six words.

a Manchester United ....usually.... play on
   Saturdays.

b Alex .... spends Saturday with his
   children.

c When Alex is at a game, his wife Liz
   .... stays with the children.

d .... , Alex doesn't play with the
   children on Sunday.

e On Saturdays, the children .... do
   puzzles and watch TV.

f Manchester United .... play in Italy.

6 Look at the pictures *1–14*. Match them with the words *a–n*. Tick (✓) the actions you do and write how often you do them.

a play football   [   ]   .....I never play football..

b go shopping   [   ]   ....

c do puzzles   [   ]   ....

d go running   [   ]   ....

e listen to music   [   ]   ....

f go to the cinema   [   ]   ....

g read   [   ]   ....

h play golf   [   ]   ....

i work out   [   ]   ....

j play tennis   [   ]   ....

k go swimming   [   ]   ....

l go skiing   [   ]   ....

m play video games   [   ]   ....

n watch TV   [   ]   ....

7 Fill in the words for you. Use the words in the box.

never   occasionally   sometimes   usually   often   always

a I .... watch football on TV.

b I .... go to the cinema at weekends.

c I .... do puzzles.

d I .... play tennis.

e I .... go running.

f I .... listen to music in the mornings.

g On Saturdays, I .... go swimming.

8 Write what you do at the weekends.

On Saturdays I often .... and I usually

.... I sometimes .... and

I always .... Occasionally I .... ,

but I never ....

••B Writing Letters

1 Look at the picture. Before you read the letter, guess the boy's:

a nationality   b job   c hobby

Hi!
I'm Lars. I'm 19 years old and I'm from Copenhagen.
My hobbies are skiing and tennis and I love watching TV. I usually go skiing on Saturdays. I've got three sisters, Birgit, Mathilde and Magda. I am a student at the University of Copenhagen.
Write to me and tell me about you.

Lars

Read the letter and check your answers.

2 Read the letter again and answer the questions.

a What's the writer's name?
b How old is he?
c Where is he from?
d What does he do in his free time?
e Has he got brothers and sisters?
f What does he do?

3 Write the sentences from the letter that answer these questions.

a What's your name? _I'm Lars._

b How old are you? ....

c Where are you from? ....

d What are your hobbies? ....

e What do you usually do on Saturdays?

....

f What do you play? ....

g How many brothers and sisters have you got? ....

h What do you do? ....

4 Read the letter again and complete the form for Lars.

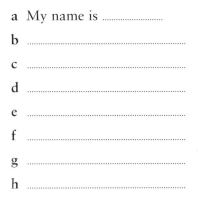

MyFace

a Name: ....

b Age: ....

c Home town: ....

d Family: ....

e Hobbies: ....

5 Answer the questions in Activity 3 for you.

a My name is ....

b ....

c ....

d ....

e ....

f ....

g ....

h ....

6 Now use your answers to Activity 5 to write your own letter to Lars.

Hi Lars!

My name is ....

....

....

....

....

....

.... ,

Write soon,

....

UNIT 8

HOW DO YOU FEEL?

•••A Reading Lifestyle

1 Match *a–g* with *1–7* to find seven activities. Then tick (✓) the ones you do.

a eating
b watching
c going
d playing
e eating
f working
g doing

1 swimming   [ ]
2 puzzles   [ ]
3 fruit   [a]
4 beefburgers   [ ]
5 out   [ ]
6 video games   [ ]
7 television   [ ]

2 Write the activities in Activity 1 in two lists: things that are good for you and things that are bad for you. Add two more of your own.

Things that are good for you	Things that are bad for you
eating fruit	eating beefburgers

3 Now answer this quiz for yourself. Check your answers at the bottom of the page.

How often do you ...

1 exercise?
A every day
B three or four times a week
C once a week
D never

4 go out with friends?
A every day
B once or twice a week
C once a month
D never

2 watch television?
A two to five hours a week
B five to ten hours a week
C ten to 20 hours a week
D more than 20 hours a week

5 eat good food?
A always
B sometimes
C usually
D never

3 relax with a book or a puzzle?
A every day
B once a week
C twice a week
D never

Count up your answers:

A .... B .... C .... D ....

4 Look at the quiz in Activity 3 and the answers. Make sentences about what it says.

Example: The quiz says exercise is good for you.
         The quiz says watching a lot of television is bad for you.

....

....

....

....

....

....

5 Read your sentences in Activity 4. Write *I agree* (☺) or *I disagree* (☹)
next to each one.

Quiz answers

Mostly A answers: You are very healthy. You eat well, you exercise and you relax. This is good for you.

Mostly B answers: You are healthy, but you need to do more exercise and eat more good food. You need to see friends more and relax more.

Mostly C answers: You are not very healthy. Do you watch a lot of television? This is bad for you. How often do you read or exercise? Food is also very important.

Mostly D answers: Your life is not healthy. It is important to exercise often and to eat good food. It is also healthy to see your friends and to relax.

B Writing Reports and graphs

1 How often do you exercise? Tick (✓) the correct answer.

never [   ]   occasionally [   ]   sometimes [   ]   often [   ]

2 Read the report and write the numbers on the bar chart.

> In our group ten people often exercise. Six people sometimes exercise and two people occasionally exercise. One person never exercises.

How often do you exercise?

Often	.....10....
Sometimes	....
Occasionally	....
Never	....

3 Read the report again and answer the questions.

a How many people exercise often? ....10...

b How often do six people exercise? ....

c How many people exercise occasionally? ....

d How many people never exercise? ....

4 Look at the results of this survey. Fill in the blanks in sentences *a–f*.

	Often	Sometimes	Occasionally	Never
1 How often do you eat beefburgers?	II	IIIII	IIIIII	I
2 How often do you eat fruit?	IIIII	III	IIII	II

a In this group, two people often eat ......*beefburgers*...... .

b Two people .... eat fruit.

c Four people occasionally eat ....

d Five people .... eat beefburgers.

e Three people .... eat ....

f One person .... eats beefburgers.

5 Draw a bar chart and write a report about the survey in Activity 4.

In this group, two people...........

....

....

....

....

....

....

SHOPPING

••A Reading Shop signs

1 Match the products *1–12* with the correct names *a–i*.

a book [9]

b cake [ ]

c camera [ ]

d dress [ ]

e fish [ ]

f magazine [ ]

g meat [ ]

h mobile phone [ ]

i MP3 player [ ]

j newspaper [ ]

k shoes [ ]

l vegetables [ ]

2 Write the names of the products under the right heading or headings.

Clothes	Food	Entertainment	Information
dress			

3 Look at these shop signs. Read the sentences *a–g*. Are they True (T) or False (F)?

a You can buy fresh milk every day at John's.   [F]

b The supermarket is open 24 hours.   [ ]

c At the dairy, there is fresh bread every day.   [ ]

d Luigi's has French shoes for men.   [ ]

e You can buy mobile phones at Camon.   [ ]

f You go to Between the Lines for old and new clothes.   [ ]

g There are special offers every day at Marshall's.   [ ]

4 Look at the shop signs again. Write at least one thing you can buy in each shop.

Luigi's – shoes...

....

....

....

....

....

5 Read these situations. Look at the shop signs again. Which shop(s) do you need?

a It's 9.00 p.m. and you need milk. ....

b You want to buy a pair of shoes for your father. ....

c You want to buy a pair of shoes for your sister. ....

d You need to buy an English book. ....

e You want to buy a news magazine. ....

f It's 2.30 p.m. and you need cheese. ....

g You need a birthday present for your brother. He's 21. ....

h You need bread. It's 10.00 p.m. on Sunday.

....

i You need bread. It's 5.00 p.m. on Friday.

....

j You need a new T-shirt. ....

6 Read these statements. Tick (✓) if they are true for you or change the statement.

a I ~~love~~ going shopping for clothes.   [ ]

   I hate going shopping for clothes.

b I like reading. I often buy newspapers and magazines.   [ ]

c I never go to camera stores.   [ ]

d I buy fresh bread every day.   [ ]

e I sometimes buy Italian shoes.   [ ]

f I don't like supermarkets.   [ ]

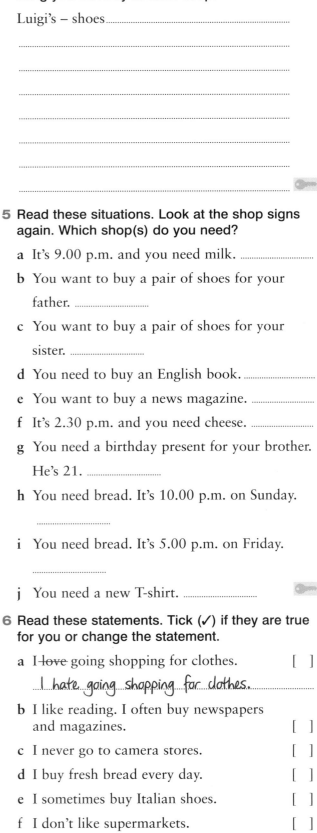

Luigi's
Italian shoes for men

Between the Lines
Old and new books –
if we don't have it
we can order it.

John's
Newspapers and
magazines

Camon **The Camera store**
Buy all your photographic equipment here.

MARSHALL'S
Clothes and shoes for all the family
Special offers every day!

SUPERMARKET
Open 24 hours
Local and imported products

KL *Bakery*
Fresh bread every day (except Sunday)
Birthday cakes are our speciality.

SUE'S DAIRY
Fresh milk and cheese every day
7.00 a.m – 3.00 p.m

•B Writing Description

1 What is your favourite piece of clothing? Choose from the words in the box.

> dress jacket pair of jeans shirt shoes skirt
> socks suit sweater tie T-shirt trousers

2 Answer the questions about your favourite piece of clothing.

a What's your favourite piece of clothing?

...... T-shirt ......

b What colour is it? ....

c Is it old or new? ....

d Is it big or small? ....

e Is it cheap or expensive? ....

f Is it warm or cool? ....

3 Write about your favourite piece of clothing. Use some of these adjectives.

> beautiful big cheap comfortable cool
> elegant expensive new old soft warm

Example: I love my red sweater. It's warm and comfortable.

4 Read the letter from a fashion magazine. Read sentences a–e and circle the correct word.

> My favourite piece of clothing is a pair of jeans. I wear them all the time. They are now very old and almost white! They are very comfortable and they look very good. I really like them and at only £25, they are my best buy ever.
>
> John, 22, London

a John's favourite piece of clothing is a pair of (jeans) / trousers.

b John wears them *often / occasionally*.

c They are *old / new*.

d They are very *elegant / comfortable*.

e They are *expensive / cheap*.

5 Read the letter again and answer the questions.

a What is the letter about? ....

b How many times is the word *jeans* used in the letter? ....

c Which two words are used instead of *jeans*?

- Which word is used as the <u>subject</u> of a sentence? Write an example.

....

....

- Which word is used as the <u>object</u> of a sentence? Write an example.

....

....

6 Write a text about 'My favourite piece of clothing for a wedding or a special day'.

Example: My favourite piece of clothing for a wedding or a special day is a ....

....

....

....

•••• A Reading Postcards

San José

1 a Look at the postcards. What country is Paula in? And Steve? Choose from the list.

a USA ....

b Brazil ....

c Mexico ....

d UK (United Kingdom) ....

1 b Read the postcards quickly and circle the correct answers.

a Who is working? *Paula/Steve*

b Who is on holiday? *Paula/Steve*

2 Read the postcards again. Read the sentences a–h, then write Paula (P) or Steve (S).

a This person is writing at a desk. [P]

b This person is sitting in the sun. [ ]

c This person is watching the sea. [ ]

d This person is eating a sandwich. [ ]

e This person is learning a lot. [ ]

f This person is having a Mexican meal. [ ]

g This person thinks San José is nice. [ ]

h This person thinks Cancún is fun. [ ]

Dear Ed,
I'm writing this postcard at my desk at the office with a sandwich in my hand. I'm learning a lot about the company but I haven't got time for fun! San José is nice.
Wish you were here!
Paula

Edward Li...
46 Church Rd
Guildford,
Surrey GU12 5LJ
England

Cancún

Hi!
This place is fun! I'm sitting in the sun, watching the sea and having a delicious Mexican meal. And I'm thinking of you!
Take care!
Steve

Evelyn Lloyd
12 Abingdon Rd
Milton Keynes
MK3 2PT
England

3 Read the postcards again and find these words in the text.
Write the words under the right heading. Then add four words
of your own.

| company   desk   office   sea   sun |

Work	Holidays
desk	

4 Fill in the blanks in the sentences.

a Paula is ....*writing*........ to Edward.

b She is .... at a desk at the office.

c Steve is .... in the sun.

d Paula is .... a sandwich.

e Steve is .... the sea.

f Steve is .... a meal.

g Steve is .... of Evelyn.

5 Write true sentences with phrases from the box. What two things
are the same for Steve and Paula?

Example: Steve is ... .

           Paula is ... .

| at the office   eating   having fun   in a nice place   learning new things |
| on holiday   working   writing to Edward |

●●●B Writing Postcards

1 Look at the postcards on page 32. Find expressions to complete the information in the table.

Opening phrase	Describing the place	Saying goodbye
Hello!	(c)	Love
(a) ...._Dear_........	(d)	(e) ....
(b)	(*name of place*) is beautiful/great!	(f) ....

2 Now read Linda's postcard to Ben and fill in the blanks. Use words from the box.

afternoon   care   ~~Dear~~   having   nice
listening   sea   swimming   taking   writing

(a) _Dear_ Ben,

Miami is great! I'm (b) .... this postcard in the car and (c) .... to music on my MP3 player. We're driving to the (d) .... – we usually go (e) .... in the morning and in the (f) .... we relax! We're (g) .... a (h) .... time here. I'm (i) .... lots of photos – this place is beautiful!

Take (j) .... ,

Linda

Ben Jones

4 Lyndhurst Road

Exmouth

EX3 5NT

UK

3 You are on holiday. Write a postcard to a friend from a place in your country. Use the expressions in Activity 1.

●●A Reading Instant messaging

1 Look at the picture. Where are the people and what are they doing?

They are in:

a a cafeteria [ ]

b an office [ ]

c a street. [ ]

2 Read the text. Which person in the picture is a) Brian, b) Johnno and c) Ryan?

a ....

b ....

c ....

File Edit View Actions Help

Bri87: hi jody! ☺

JJ20: hi brian! where ru?

Bri87: in the cafeteria

JJ20: what ru doing?

Bri87: having my lunch

JJ20: busy?

Bri87: not really. i'm watching people

JJ20: who's there?

Bri87: u know John Murray? *Johnno*?

JJ20: yes

Bri87: he's just coming in – funny guy!

JJ20: what's he wearing today?

Bri87: big red T-shirt and red trousers – looks like a tomato!

JJ20: LOL☺he always wears funny clothes. who's with him?

Bri87: ryan

JJ20: ryan? description?

Bri87: tall, dark hair, dark eyes – always wears a cap

JJ20: long, wavy hair?

Bri87: that's him

JJ20: good-looking guy!

Bri87: u like him? ❤

JJ20: maybe. ☺

Bri87: K – they're coming

JJ20: K – bye, brian

Bri87: cu

⊗ Block   A Font   ☺ ▾ Emoticons

3 Answer the questions.

a Where is Brian?   *in the cafeteria*

b What is he doing?   ....

c What is John Murray wearing?   ....

d Why does he look like a tomato?   ....

e What does Ryan look like?   ....

f What does Ryan always wear?   .... 🔑

4 Match the words and expressions *a–i* with the IM (instant messaging) language *1–9*.

a Do you like him?   1 K

b OK.   2 busy?

c I'm laughing.   3 u like him?

d See you.   4 description?

e What does he look like?   5 where ru?

f What are you doing?   6 u know John Murray?

g Do you know John Murray?   7 LOL

h Where are you?   8 cu

i Are you busy?   9 what ru doing? 🔑

5 Fill in the blanks in this conversation. You are *browneyes 1* and your friend is *longhair 2*. Talk about your classroom.

File   Edit   View   Actions   Help

browneyes 1: hi

longhair 2: ....

browneyes 1: where ru?

longhair 2: ....

browneyes 1: What ru doing?

longhair 2: ....

browneyes 1: Busy?

longhair 2: ....

browneyes 1: Who's there ?

longhair 2: ....

browneyes 1: What's happening?

longhair 2: ....

🚫 Block   A Font   😊 ▾ Emoticons

•B Writing Descriptions

1 Look at the pictures. Write words under the correct heading.

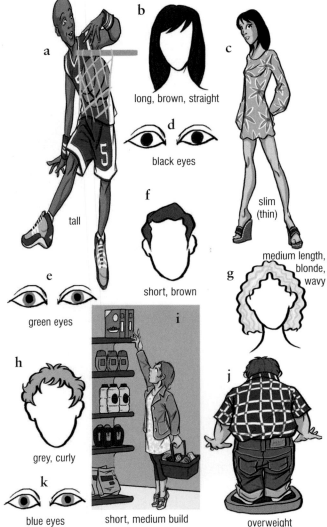

a tall

b long, brown, straight

c slim (thin)

d black eyes

e green eyes

f short, brown

g medium length, blonde, wavy

h grey, curly

i short, medium build

j overweight (chubby, fat)

k blue eyes

Eyes	Hair	Body
blue		

2 Look at the three women and fill in the blanks in these descriptions.

a I'm _medium height_ and .... I have short .... hair and .... eyes. Today, I'm wearing a blue .... and a blue ....

b I'm .... and quite .... I have short .... hair and .... eyes. Today I'm wearing white .... , a black .... and a red and yellow ....

c I'm .... and .... I have long .... hair and brown .... Today I'm wearing brown .... , blue .... and a green ....

3 Imagine you have to get someone from the airport. This person doesn't know you. Write an email describing yourself. Put the information in the same order as in paragraphs a–c in Activity 2.

•••A Reading Ads

1 How do you keep in contact? <u>Match the pictures a–f with the words 1–6 on the right. Then(circle)the ones you use.</u>

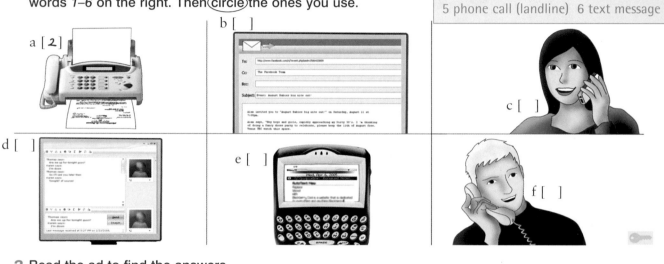

a [2]   b [ ]   c [ ]   d [ ]   e [ ]   f [ ]

2 Read the ad to find the answers.

a The ad is for *a comfortable bed / a mobile phone*.
b The ad is for *busy people / fashion writers*.

Phonewhiz

Nicole is a busy person. She works for a magazine. She writes articles about fashion. She has important meetings every day.

Today, Nicole is in bed with a cold. So, is she just having a rest? No, she's working. She's writing a new article. She's making phone calls, texting people, sending emails and choosing photos on the Internet – all from her comfortable bed.

And she's even listening to music, too!

With **Phonewhiz** you are always in contact.

Phonewhiz – *because life doesn't stop when you are not in the office.*

3 Read the ad in Activity 2 again, and look at the list *1–6* in Activity 1. Which things are in the ad? Tick (✓) them in the list. Which things are not in the ad? Put a cross (✗) in the list.

4 Read the ad again and write True (T) or False (F).

a Nicole is not a very busy person.   [F]

b She writes articles about fashion for a magazine.   [ ]

c Nicole is having a rest today.   [ ]

d She's writing a new article for the magazine today.   [ ]

e Her bed is not very comfortable.   [ ]

f She is watching TV too.   [ ]

5 Read the ad again. Answer the questions.

a What does Nicole write about? ......fashion..........

b What does Nicole do with other people every day? ....

c Where is Nicole working today? ....

d What is wrong with Nicole? ....

e What three things is Nicole doing to keep in contact? ....

f What is she doing to relax? ....

6 Complete the sentence about you. Choose one of the ideas in the box.

I would / would not like to have a Phonewhiz because

....

```
... it's very useful.

... I don't always want to be in contact.

... I always want to be in contact.

... I don't want to work when I am ill.
```

7 Read these sentences. Circle three things you are doing now. Then write them below.

I'm working.
I'm having a rest.
I'm writing something.
I'm listening to music.
I'm very busy.
I'm not very busy.
I'm watching TV.
I'm texting someone.
I'm making a phone call.
I'm watching TV.
I'm reading my English book.

I'm ....

....

....

•••B Writing Emails

1 Read the email. Answer the questions. Which question is it not possible to answer?

a Who is the email from?

Peter Steele

b Who is the email for?

....

c What is the email about?

....

d Who is organising the club? ....

e What's the date?

....

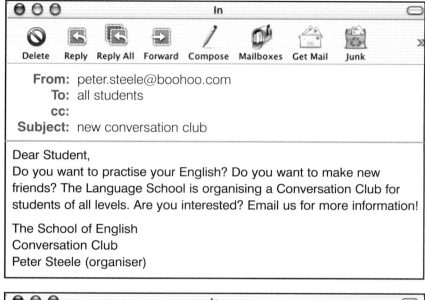

From: peter.steele@boohoo.com
To: all students
cc:
Subject: new conversation club

Dear Student,
Do you want to practise your English? Do you want to make new friends? The Language School is organising a Conversation Club for students of all levels. Are you interested? Email us for more information!

The School of English
Conversation Club
Peter Steele (organiser)

2 Read the email from José Bondia, who is interested in the Club and has Elementary level English, but would like more information. Fill in the blanks.

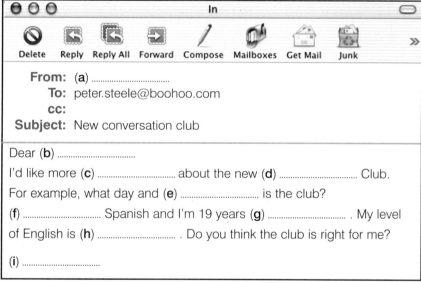

From: (a) ....
To: peter.steele@boohoo.com
cc:
Subject: New conversation club

Dear (b) ....

I'd like more (c) .... about the new (d) .... Club.

For example, what day and (e) .... is the club?

(f) .... Spanish and I'm 19 years (g) .... My level

of English is (h) .... Do you think the club is right for me?

(i) ....

3 You are interested in the Conversation Club but you want more information. Write an email to the organiser.

– Ask about the days and the time.

– Say why you are learning English and how often you have lessons.

– Ask if the club is right for you.

From:
To: peter.steele@boohoo.com
cc:
Subject: New conversation club

A Reading Homes

1 Match the words for rooms in the house *a–e* with the pictures *1–5*.

a bathroom   [5]

b living room   [   ]

c bedroom   [   ]

d kitchen   [   ]

e dining room   [   ]

2 Complete the sentences with the words from Activity 1.

a At home, we cook in the big ....*kitchen*........ .

b We usually watch TV in the ....

c My brother and I sleep in one ....

d There is a .... next to my bedroom with a shower.

e On Sundays, the family eats in the ....

3 Read the ads on page 42 and match the ads to the pictures. Which ad hasn't got a picture?

a ☐

b ■

c ■

1

GREAT FLAT on 6th floor. Large kitchen, small dining room, living room, four bedrooms and three bathrooms. Balcony. Only £1,200 per week. No pets. Call 364728 to see it.

2

Large house in the country for rent. Four bedrooms, two bathrooms, large dining room, large kitchen. Perfect for a family. £1,500 per month. Get keys from J. Beal Office 9.00 a.m. – 5.00 p.m.

3

FOR RENT: small house in city centre – two bedrooms, kitchen, living room/dining room, bathroom. Near the shops. £400 per week. Write to rent@accommodation.net for appointment.

4

FLAT FOR RENT: £300 per week for one bedroom, perfect for a couple. Small kitchen, living room/dining room, bathroom. Opposite station. Call 463849.

4 Read the ads agains and circle the correct word.

a   The large house has four *bedrooms* / *bathrooms*.

b   The small house is *near* / *opposite* shops.

c   The 6th-floor flat has a large *dining room* / *kitchen*.

d   The one-bedroom flat is perfect for a *couple* / *family*.

5 Complete this table about the ads.

	Ad 1:	Ad 2:	Ad 3:	Ad 4:
House or flat?				
Price?				
Location?				
No. of bedrooms?				
No. of bathrooms?				

6 Which place do you like? Why?

I like the .... because it's ......*big*....... . It is perfect for

....

It has ....

and it's ....

B Writing Lost property

1 Read the web page and underline information *a–d* in the letter.

LONDON LOST PROPERTY

Home | **News** | **Contact us** | **Sitemap**

If you lose something in London, send an email to London Lost Property:
lost@londonlostproperty.co.uk.

You must include:
a the date   **b** the time   **c** where   **d** what

For example:

I am writing to you because I lost my black umbrella on the number 52 bus in London. I lost it on Monday August 16 at about 3 o'clock in the afternoon.

Constance Bradshaw
cbradshaw@yiphee.co.uk

2 Read the web page again and fill in the blanks.

Constance lost her (**a**) *black umbrella* . She lost it on the (**b**) .... bus in (**c**) .... on Monday (**d**) .... at about (**e**) .... o'clock in the (**f**) ....

3 These people have lost these things. Read the table. Choose two things and write two emails to London Lost Property.

Who	Date	Time	Where	What
Richard Crane	August 23	5.30 p.m.	number 73 bus	tie
Emma Davis	April 14	9.00 a.m.	Trafalgar Square	mobile phone
Rory O'Brien	March 13	8.30 a.m.	Green Park	watch

From: Richard Crane
To: lost@londonlostproperty.co.uk
cc:
Subject: Lost tie

FINDING THINGS

●●●A Reading San Francisco

Come to San Francisco!

The city has everything. First of all, there is the world-famous Golden Gate Bridge and of course there is another bridge – the Bay Bridge goes across the bay to the cities of Oakland, Berkeley and Emeryville.

If you're looking for shops, San Francisco is the place for you. There are great shops and shopping centres.

Do you need a place to stay? There are 32,866 hotel rooms in town – so you can find the perfect one for you.

Parks? There are many parks in San Francisco including the famous Golden Gate Park. In the park there is a Japanese Tea Garden, a rose garden and a lake.

Are you hungry? San Francisco has great restaurants – French, Italian, Japanese, Chinese, Mexican, Argentinian and more.

There are lots of great museums, too: The MOMA (Museum of Modern Art), the Asian Art Museum, the Exploratorium and many more.

Architecture? Don't miss the 'Painted Ladies': a row of brightly painted old houses, but there are beautiful houses all over the city.

For entertainment there are many bars and clubs – people are never bored in San Francisco.

1 Look at the title and the pictures. What do you know about this place?

  a What state in the USA is it in? ....

  b Is it near the sea? ....

  c What is the name of its famous bridge? ....

2 Read the text. Match and complete the captions for photos 1, 2 and 3.

  a These are the 'Painted Ladies', a row of brightly painted ....　　[   ]

  b This is the .... in the famous ....　　[   ]

  c This is the world-famous Golden ....　　[   ]

3 Complete this table about San Francisco with information from the text.

a	Number of bridges:	2
b	Number of hotel rooms:	
c	Attractions in Golden Gate Park:	
d	Types of restaurants:	
e	Names of museums:	

4 Read the text again and write True (T) or False (F).

a There are two bridges in San Francisco.   [T]

b There are great shops and shopping centres.   [ ]

c There is a Chinese tea garden in the Golden Gate Park.   [ ]

d There aren't any French restaurants.   [ ]

e The 'Painted Ladies' are brightly painted old hotels.   [ ]

f For entertainment, there are bars but not many clubs.   [ ]

5 Rewrite the false sentences.

....

....

....

....

6 Read these sentences and fill in the blanks with words from the text.

a There is a park near our house with a beautiful rose ....

b We often go swimming in the .... near here.

c There is a great .... in our town with lots of modern art paintings.

d We always stay in a beautiful .... in the centre of town.

e We're eating a meal in our favourite Mexican ....

7 Make a list of the places in San Francisco. Write them under the correct heading.

Parks	Types of restaurants	Art galleries	Bridges
Golden Gate Park	....	....	....
....	....	....	....
....	....	....	....

8 Would you like to visit San Francisco? Why or why not?

I would like to visit San Francisco because I love going shopping and

....

....

....

●●●B Writing Travel brochure

Come to Exmouth, Devon in sunny South West England!

Exmouth has everything. First of all, there is the famous beach. Then there's the market, shops and gardens.

Are you hungry? Exmouth has some nice restaurants. There is a great fish restaurant and there are Chinese and Indian restaurants too and more.

Do you need a place to stay? There are hotel rooms in town.

Are you interested in architecture? Don't miss the town hall, a beautiful old building.

For entertainment, there is a cinema, a small museum and a swimming pool; there are also lots of pubs and bars.

There is a train station and it is only 25 minutes to Exeter City.

People are never bored in Exmouth!

1 Read the brochure about Exmouth and answer the questions.

a Is there a market in the town?

Yes, there is.

b Is there a bridge?

c Are there any hotels?

d Are there any restaurants?

e Are there any beautiful old buildings?

f What is there for entertainment?

2 Make a list of all the important things to see and do in Exmouth.

3 Answer the questions in Activity 1 for your town.

a Is there a market in the town?

No, there isn't.

b

c

d

e

f

4 Make a list of all the important things to see and do in your town or city.

Example: *Important things to see: ...*
Facilities: ...

5 Write a text for a brochure about your home town.

Come to .... in .... !

.... has everything. First of all, there is ....

What photographs would you put in the brochure?

CAN YOU PLAY THE PIANO?

••A Reading A jazz musician

1 Unjumble the words and find seven musical instruments. Write them in the right place in the grid. Which instrument does not fit?

a pettrum
b noopsaxhe
c anopi
d livino
e smudr
f neticarl
g ratuig

		¹T					
		R			³		
²	R	U	S		A		
		M					
		⁴P	I		N	O	
		E			P		⁵G
		T					
	⁶	L	R		E	T	
					E		

Answer: .... does not fit in the grid.

•••B Writing *and, but, so*

ON THE ROAD The traveller's website

Home ▌ News ▌ Classifieds ▌ Your stories ▌ Contact us

Send your travel stories to us!

Dallas to Acapulco

I didn't have a summer job, so I decided to look through the job ads. I saw an ad for a driver to go from Dallas, Texas to Acapulco, Mexico and rang the number. Carlos, a mechanic, wanted help with the driving and some money for the petrol. He was a friendly guy, so I decided to go with him. It was a long trip, but we had fun. My girlfriend was on holiday in Acapulco, so I met her there. It was a great holiday, but it was really cheap!

---

1 Read the story on the travellers' website. Match the beginning of the sentences *a–g* with the correct ending *1–7*.

a I didn't have a summer job, **so**

b It was a long trip, **but**

c Carlos wanted help with the driving **and**

d It was a great holiday, **but**

e I saw an ad for a driver **and**

f My girlfriend was on holiday in Acapulco, **so**

g Carlos was a friendly guy, **so**

1 I met her there.

2 some money for the petrol.

3 I decided to go with him.

4 rang the number.

5 it was really cheap!

6 I decided to look through the job ads.

7 we had fun.

KEY
and joins two similar ideas
but joins two contrasting ideas
so says what happened as a result of something else

2 Read the box then complete the statements *a–c* with *and, but* or *so*.

a The word .... introduces the result of a situation or activity.

b We don't have to repeat the subject after .... when it is the same in the second part of the sentence.

c We use a comma before .... and ....

3 Complete the sentences about a trip you took.

a I went to ...., but ....

b We visited .... and ....

c I don't like travelling alone, so ....

d It was a long/short trip, but ....

e I didn't have a lot of money, so ....

f The hotel was nice and ....

4 Write a full paragraph about your trip. Include the sentences *a–f*.

....

....

HOPES AND PLANS

••A Reading Treasure hunt

1 Read the article. Choose the best title.

a Treasure hunting around the world   [   ]
b Explore new places   [   ]
c Fun and games around the world   [   ] 🔑

> I met Jeff and Vicky on a plane to Italy. 'We are going to the island of Capri,' Jeff said. 'We are going to look for treasure.' Treasure? On Capri? Jeff explained: 'It's not real treasure. It's a game called *Geocache*. It's like a treasure hunt.' That's how I first heard of *Geocache*. To play, you register on an Internet site. It's free. To hide your treasure (or cache), you put it in a plastic box – any object you want – with a pen and a notebook (the logbook). Then you fill in a form online with coordinates to help people find it. People look up caches on the Internet and then go and find them, anywhere in the world. When you find a cache, you can take the prize in the box and leave another prize. You record your discovery in the logbook and you hide the cache again. 'We hope we can find a cache on Capri during our holiday,' says Jeff. 'It's a good way to explore new places and make new friends.'

2 Read the article again and put the following instructions in the correct order.

a When you find a cache take the prize in the box and leave another prize.   [   ]

b Next, you hide your treasure in a plastic box. Put a pen and notebook in the box too.   [   ]

c First, you register on an Internet site.   [1]

d Finally, you hide the cache again.   [   ]

e You fill in a form online with coordinates to help people find it.   [   ]

f You record your discovery in a logbook.   [   ] 🔑

●●● B Writing Instructions

1 Number the pictures *a–f* to show how to use the washing machine.

....   *1 put in (clothes)*

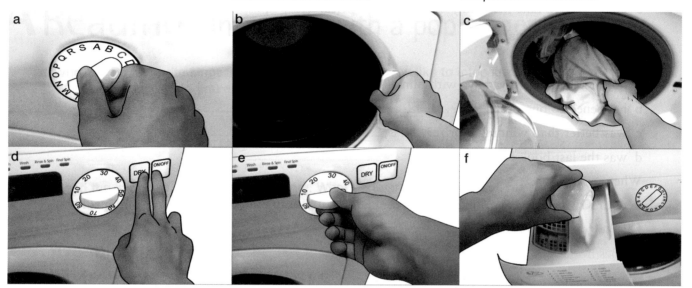

....

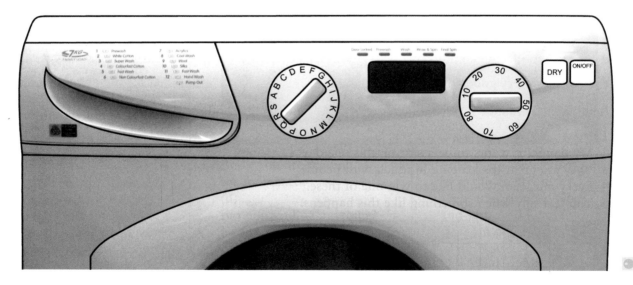

Then match the verbs in the box with the pictures *a–f*.

> choose (programme)   put in (detergent/clothes)
> shut (door)   press (button)   set (time)

2 Write a set of instructions for a friend staying in your house.

How to use the washing machine
1. Put the clothes in.
2. ....

Answer key

Unit 1

A

1 a I'm Tom. What's your name?
  b Nice to meet you.
  c I'm Mike.
  d Not bad, thank you.
2 1 Yoshi Watanabe
  2 Elena Petrovich
  3 Roseni Amorim
  4 Charlie Walker
3 a Roseni
  b Elena
  c Yoshi
  d Elena, Yoshi
  e Yoshi, Charlie
  f Charlie
4 1 b
  2 a
  3 c
  4 d
5 f, a, b, e, d, c, g

B

1 a Jerome
  b David, Ray
  c Jane, Jaro
  d Nick
2 a F
  b T
  c T
  d F
3 a4 b6 c3 d1 e5 f2
4 a What's your name?
  b How are you?
  c Who are your friends?
  d Are you a student?
  e Who is your teacher?

Unit 2

A

1 **Colours:** grey, blue, yellow, black, green, white, red
  Countries: United Kingdom, Mexico, France, Australia, Canada, Japan
  Nationalities: Mexican, Canadian, French, Japanese, Australian, British
2 a4 b3 c1 d8 e2 f6 g5 h7
3 a F
  b F
  c T
  d T
  e T
  f F
  g T

4 1 They're from Japan. / They're Japanese.
  2 They're from China. / They're Chinese.
  3 He's from Australia. / He's Australian.
  4 They're from the United Kingdom. / They're British.
  5 She's from Russia. / She's Russian.
  6 They're from Mexico. / They're Mexican.
  7 They're from Brazil. / They're Brazilian.
  8 They're from the United States. / They're American.
5 a His name is Jonno
  b No, he isn't.
  c Yes, he is.
  d He's from Australia.
  e Yes, it is.

B

1 a Canadian
  b Westchester
  c from Canada
  d Chinese
2 a How are you?
  b Are you British?
  c Where are you from?
  d Is it nice?
3 I'm very well, thank you.
  I'm British but my dad is Russian.
  We're from Bakewell, near Manchester.
  And yes, Bakewell is nice.

Unit 3

A

1 a kitchen
  b hospital
  c hospital
  d theatre
  e office
  f street
  g theatre
  h office
  i theatre
  j school
2 Stephanie: a school, teacher
  Alex: a theatre, dancer
  Andrew: a kitchen, cook
  Patrick: an office, architect

3 a F
  b F
  c F
  d T
  e T
4 a Stephanie
  b Andrew
  c Alex
  d Patrick
5 a baker
  b dancer
  c bus driver
  d computer programmer
  e painter

B

1 a F
  b F
  c F
  d F
  e T
2 a Lola
  b Moreno
  c ?
  d Spain
  e morenolola@aol.com
  f yes
  g 07856 563387
  h computer programmer

Unit 4

A

10 words
italic = male
bold = female

80   Answer key

86   Notes